Guide to

Handling Bereavement

The Easyway

Adrian Lewis

Easyway Guides

British Library Cataloguing in Publication Data. A catalogue record is available for this book from the British Library.

ISBN

978-1-84716-844-3

Printed and bound by 4edge www.4edge.co.uk

Cover design by Bookworks Islington

Whilst every effort has been taken to ensure that the information contained in this book was accurate at the time of going to print, the publisher and the author cannot accept any liability for any inaccuracies contained within or for changes in legislation since writing the book.

CONTENTS

Introduction

Introduction

Death is an unpleasant reality and one that many people avoid thinking about. However, on the death of a person who is close there are very necessary actions that need to be taken. This book, updated to **2018**, and which now includes probate in Scotland and Northern Ireland, is an attempt to enlighten the reader as to the practical steps that need to be taken after the death of a person. Each step is outlined along with the role of the funeral director and the role of the church and crematoria after death.

The role of the coroner is outlined and also the doctor, registrar, clergymen and cemetery and crematorium officials. This book does not dwell in depth on bereavement counseling, as this is a separate area and warrants a book on its own. It does, however, outline the process of grief and discuss aspects of this and offers advice in a limited way. The book is very much a practical guide and has been written in the hope that people may benefit from it at this difficult time.

There is a section on non-Christian burial in the recognition that the United Kingdom is a diverse multi-racial society and different traditions apply to different cultures. There is also a section on wills and probate, as dealing with an estate after death can be very complex and time consuming, particularly if there is no will. Finally, there is a list of useful addresses at the end of the book. Before we look at the practical side of handling death we will look at bereavement generally.

Bereavement generally

Bereavement affects people in different ways. There's no right or wrong way to feel. You might feel a lot of emotions at once, or feel you're having a good day, then you wake up and feel worse again. Experts generally accept that there are four stages of bereavement:

- accepting that your loss is real
- experiencing the pain of grief
- adjusting to life without the person who has died
- putting less emotional energy into grieving and putting it into something new (in other words, moving on)

You'll probably go through all these stages, but you won't necessarily move smoothly from one to the next. Your grief might feel chaotic and out of control, but these feelings will eventually become less intense. Give yourself time, as they will pass. You might feel:

- shock and numbness (this is usually the first reaction to the death, and people often speak of being in a daze)
- overwhelming sadness, with lots of crying
- tiredness or exhaustion
- anger, for example towards the person who died, their illness or God
- guilt, for example guilt about feeling angry, about something you said or didn't say, or about not being able to stop your loved one dying

These feelings are all perfectly normal. Lots of people feel guilty about their anger, but it's natural to be angry and to question why.

The GOV.UK website has information on what to do after someone dies, such as registering the death and planning a funeral. Throughout this book we will make reference to this site.

Coping with grief

Talking and sharing your feelings with someone can help. Don't go through this alone. For some people, relying on family and friends is the best way to cope. But if you don't feel you can talk to them much (perhaps you aren't close, or they're grieving too), you can contact local bereavement services through your GP, local hospice, or the National Cruse helpline on 0808 808 1677.

A bereavement counsellor can give you time and space to talk about your feelings, including the person who has died, your relationship, family, work, fears and the future. You can have access to a bereavement counsellor at any time, even if the person you lost died a long time ago.

Don't be afraid to talk about the person who has died. People in your life might not mention their name because they don't want to upset you. But if you feel you can't talk to them, it can make you feel isolated.

If you need help to move on

Each bereavement is unique, and you can't tell how long it will last. In general, the death and the person might not constantly be at the forefront of your mind after around 18 months. This period may be shorter or longer for some people, which is normal.

Your GP or a bereavement counsellor can help if you feel that you're not coping. Some people also get support from a religious minister. You might need help if:

- you can't get out of bed
- you neglect yourself or your family, for example you don't eat properly
- you feel you can't go on without the person you've lost
- the emotion is so intense it's affecting the rest of your life, for example you can't face going to work or you're taking your anger out on someone else

These feelings are normal as long as they don't last for a long time. The time to get help depends on the person, if these things last for a period that you feel is too long, or your family say they're worried, that's the time to seek help. Your GP can refer you, and they can monitor your general health. Some people turn to alcohol or drugs during difficult times. Get help cutting down on alcohol, or see the Frank website www.talktofrank.com for information on drugs.

The Death Café Movement

Inspired by the work of Bernard Crettaz, a Swiss Sociologist, John Underwood, the Founder of the Death Café Movement created the first Temporary Death Café in 2011 in the basement of his home in London. The movement quickly spread to over 4000 temporary Cafes throughout the world.

The idea is that people can discuss all aspects of death, from the practical aspects i.e. what to do when someone dies and also sharing tales of bereavement, such as personal experiences and also ones own view of death. The overall aim is to allow people to open up about death and all that surrounds it.

To find out more and locate a Death Café near to you go to deathcafe.com

Pre-bereavement care

If someone has an incurable illness, they and their loved ones can prepare for bereavement.. Bereavement counsellors offer pre-bereavement care, helping patients and their family cope with their feelings. This can be especially important for children, children's stress levels are at their highest before their family member dies, so support during this time is important.

You can find out more about children and bereavement from the Childhood Bereavement Network. In the next chapter, we will look at the first steps involved in handling a death, this is the registration of death.

Ch.1

Death and the Registration Of Death

If you suspect a person is dead, the first thing that you should do is to tell a doctor. There may be some doubt as to whether the person has died. In all cases, call a doctor or phone the ambulance service. Ask whether the doctor is going to attend. If the death of a person has been expected, then it may not be immediately necessary for a doctor to attend late at night, the next morning will do.

If the doctor does not intend to come, for reasons made very clear, remove the body. If a decision has been made that the funeral will be a cremation, the doctor will need to know as special papers will need to be drawn up which will involve an inspection, separately, by two doctors. If you intend to keep a body at home prior to such an inspection, which can be carried out in a funeral parlour, then it will be necessary to keep the room at a cool temperature.

Laying out a body

This is the first stage in preparing a body for burial or cremation.

If carried out by a funeral director it is termed last offices, the "first office", denoting either the first or last contact. The body is washed and tidied up, eyelids closed and jaw closed. Hair is tidied, arms and legs and hair usually grows for sometime after a death so therefore will need shaving. If a funeral director is laying out a body then a gown or everyday clothes will be applied.

Although laying out and general preparation can be carried out at home, and a funeral director can also provide a service in the home, it is usual to allow the body to be taken away to a funeral parlor. An occurrence after death is Rigor Mortis, which is a stiffening of the muscles. This begins normally six hours after death and takes effect all over the body within 24 hours, after which it usually begins to wear off. In addition, about half an hour after death parts of the dead persons skin will begin to show dark patches. This activity is called Hypostasis and is due to settlement of the blood in the body due to gravity.

Police involvement

In certain circumstances it may be necessary to call the police if a persons death is not due to natural circumstances. It could be that a death is the result of murder or other suspicious circumstance. It is very important not to touch anything in the room as you may disturb vital evidence. The police will take statements from anyone who was with the person before death. There may at times be difficulty in identifying a dead body and the police have a specific procedure in this case.

Certificate of cause of death

In the United Kingdom, every death must be recorded in the local registrar's office within five days. The Registrar will always require a certificate as to the cause of death. If the cause of death is known then the doctor attending on death will provide the certificate, which states the cause, when last seen alive and whether or not any doctor has seen the body since death occurred. This certificate will be given to the family. No charge is usually made. If the doctor concerned is uncertain about the cause of death or has not seen the body for 14 days after death then a certificate cannot be issued and the coroners office is informed. The body is taken to the coroner's mortuary and a post mortem may or may not be carried out.

The coroner

A Coroner is a qualified doctor or solicitor and is paid by the local authority. The coroner is independent of both local and central government and is responsible only to the Crown. The coroner is assisted by the coroner's officer, usually a police officer. The coroner's office has contact with the public.

When a death occurs which is not due to natural causes it must be reported to the coroner. If the deceased died of natural causes but was not seen by a doctor for a significant time before death or after death then the coroner must be reported to. The deceased person's doctor will be contacted and cause of death and circumstances ascertained. If satisfied the coroner will cease involvement and issue a certificate and the family can then register the death normally. In any cases where the doctor is uncertain as to the cause of the death then the coroner must be notified. Death resulting from industrial disease, which has given rise to compensation, must be reported to the coroner. In addition, death arising from military service must be reported, in some but not all cases. Other circumstances in which death has arisen which must be reported are:

- If the death was suspicious
- Was sudden or unexplained
- Due to neglect, i.e., poisoning, drugs etc
- Caused directly or indirectly by accident
- Suicide
- In prison or police custody

18

Another situation is during surgery or before recovering from the effects of anesthetic. When a death is reported to a coroner, and an investigation is decided upon then a death cannot be registered until enquiries are complete. There will usually be a post mortem. If death is shown to be from natural causes then the family will be notified and the death can be registered normally.

The family of the deceased do not have to be consulted or asked about carrying out a post mortem. If the law requires it then the coroner has to proceed. However, if a family or individual objects they can register that objection with the coroner who has to listen and give reasons for a post mortem. If there are still objections there is the right of appeal to the High Court. This will delay disposal of the body. The coroner has no duty to inform the next of kin about findings of a post mortem. After the post mortem, and a coroner's report made to the relevant authorities, the body becomes the responsibility of the family.

The coroner is obliged to hold an inquest into every violent and unnatural death and also death whilst in prison. The inquest is open to the public and can take the form of a trial, with witnesses called. The office of the coroner is a powerful office and the intention is to ensure that death was natural and not due to

19

violent or other unnatural means. After the inquest is over then the death can be registered in the normal way.

Information concerning death, including the handing in of a certificate or the informing of the registrar of an extended period without certificate due to post mortem or other examination, can be given at any registrar's office (In England and Wales). This will then be passed on to the appropriate district or sub office.

Registration of death

As stated, in England, Wales and Northern Ireland a death should be registered within five days of occurrence (8 days in Scotland, to the Procurator Fiscal see below registering a death in Scotland). Registration can be delayed for up to another nine days if the registrar receives written confirmation that a doctor has signed a medical certificate of cause of death. The medical certificate must be presented at the register office in the sub-district where the death occurred. The person registering the death must decide how many copies of the death certificate is needed and pay for them at the office. Payment can be by cheque, or credit card if ordering online or by telephone. The registration is free. Any certified copies of death certificates will be £9.25 at the time of registration. After registration, for up to one month, the cost of a copy certificate will be £9.25. If you require a copy certificate urgently, you may wish to use the Priority Service. The cost for this service is £23.40. You can check current fees at www.gov.uk/order-copy-birth-death-marriage-certificate. there is a different process in Scotland and Northern ireland, information of which can also be obtained from the website.

If the death certificate is to be sent to someone else then the details must be given to the registrar. It is possible at this stage for what is known as the "Green certificate" authorising burial or cremation to be sent to the funeral director carrying out the funeral arrangements. Names addresses and phone numbers of local registrars can be found in doctors surgeries, libraries etc.

Registrar's requirements

Registrar's information is contained on a part of a medical certificate issued by the doctor. This part is entitled "notice to informant" and lists:

- The date and place of death
- The full name, including maiden name if appropriate of the deceased
- Date of birth
- Occupation

- Occupation of the husband if deceased was a married woman or widow
- Address
- Whether deceased was in receipt of pension or allowance from public funds
- If the deceased was married, the date of birth of the surviving partner.

The form also states that the deceased's medical card should be given to the registrar. The other side of this particular form gives details of who is qualified to inform the registrar of a death. If the death occurs in a house or any other public building, the following can inform a registrar of a death:

- A relative of the deceased who was present at the death
- A relative who was present during the last illness
- A relative of the deceased who was not present at the death or during the last illness but who lives in the district or sub-district where the death occurred
- A person who is not a relative but who was present at the time of death
- The occupier of the building where the death occurred, if aware of the details of death

- Any inmate of the building where the death occurred, if aware of the details of death
- The person causing the disposal of the body, meaning the person accepting responsibility for arranging the funeral, but not the funeral director, who cannot register the death

The above are in order of preference. If a person has been found dead elsewhere, the following are qualified to register the death:

- Any relative of the dead person able to provide the registrar with the required details
- Any person present at time of death
- The person who found the body
- The person in charge of the body (which will be the police if the body cannot be identified)
- The person accepting responsibility for arranging the funeral

Only a person qualified under the law can inform the registrar of the death. If the registrar considers that the cause of death supplied on the medical certificate is inadequate, or the death should have been reported to the coroner, the registrar must inform the coroner and wait for written authority to proceed before continuing with registration. In cases where a coroner's inquest has been held, the coroner will act as the person informing death.

The Presumption of Death Act 2013

The Presumption of Death Act, 2013, passed after years of campaigning, will allow relatives to apply for a single certificate declaring someone presumed dead, helping them resolve that person's affairs. Its creation follows a campaign by the charity Missing People, and relatives of missing people, including Peter Lawrence, father of missing chef Claudia Lawrence, and Rachel Elias, the sister of Manic Street Preachers guitarist Richey Edwards who went missing in 1995.

Their concerns were raised before the Justice Select Committee and the All-Party Parliamentary Group for Runaway and Missing Children and Adults, and the new law was passed. The new law, based on the Scottish Presumption of Death Act 1977, only allows families to apply for a presumption of death order after seven years.

Campaigners said they will continue to fight for another law on guardianship, allowing families to maintain a missing person's estate during these years by cancelling direct debits, paying off debts, and providing maintenance for dependants.

Registering a stillbirth

A stillbirth should be registered at a register office within 42 days. Sometimes a stillbirth can be registered after 42 days - the register office can explain when this can happen. You can name the baby in the register.

In Scotland you must register a stillbirth within 21 days. In Northern Ireland you have up to 1 year to register a stillbirth.

Who can register the stillbirth

If the baby's parents are married, either the mother or father can register. The mother can sign if:

- the baby's parents are not married
- the father cannot be traced or is unknown
- If both parents want the father's name in the register:
- both parents can sign the register together
- the mother can sign and bring a 'signed declaration' from the father (the register office can explain how to do this).

If the father registers the stillbirth and the parents are not married, the mother will need to make a 'signed declaration' (the register office can explain how to do this).If the child was conceived as a result of fertility treatment Either of the following can register the stillbirth:

25

- the mother
- the father, if he was married to the mother at the time of treatment
- the second female parent if she was in a civil partnership with the mother at the time of treatment

If neither parent can attend

The following people can register the stillbirth:

- the occupier of the hospital or house where the stillbirth took place
- someone who was present at the stillbirth
- someone who is responsible for the stillborn child
- the person who found the stillborn child, if the date and place of the stillbirth are unknown

What you need to take

You need the medical certificate of stillbirth issued by the doctor or midwife. You can arrange a funeral for your baby.

Financial support and taking time off work

Following a stillbirth, you're normally entitled to:

- Statutory Maternity Pay - if you're employed
- Maternity Allowance - if you're not entitled to Statutory Maternity Pay

- Maternity Leave - if you're employed
- Statutory Paternity Pay - if you're employed
- Paternity Leave - if you're employed

You will be asked for evidence to get financial support. This can be the notification for the registration of a stillbirth from the attending doctor or midwife, or a certificate of stillbirth from the registrar. You will not be able to claim Child Benefit.

Support organisations

The following organisations give support and advice:

- Sands www.sands.org.uk 0808 164 3332
- Tommy's www.tommys.org 0208 398 3400

A lot of funeral directors will give their services free of charge on such occasions, although there may be a fee for crematoria that is incurred on behalf of clients. Some hospitals offer reverent disposal of stillborn and miscarried children, which often involves a simple ceremony led by a chaplain. In such cases there may be no ashes for subsequent burial or scattering.

Death in a hospital

There is a slight difference to the procedures up to the time of

27

registration if a death is in hospital. The relatives or next of kin are informed of the death by the hospital staff. If death was unexpected, for example, the result of an operation or accident, the coroner will be involved. Usually, all deaths occurring within 24 hours of an operation will be reported to the coroner. The coroner must by law be informed of all deaths under suspicious circumstances, or death due to medical mishap, industrial disease, violence, neglect, abortion or any kind of poisoning. If the person who died was not already an in-patient in a hospital then a member of the family may be asked to identify the body.

In cases where the coroner is involved it will not be possible to issue a medical certificate of the cause of death, but in other cases this is usually issued by the hospital doctor and given to the next of kin. If the person died before the hospital doctor had the chance to diagnose the cause, then the deceased patient's own doctor may be sometimes asked to issue the medical certificate. The deceased's possessions will have to be removed from the hospital, with a receipt needing to be signed on removal. If the medical certificate of the cause of death can be signed in the hospital then relatives will have to make arrangements to remove the body from the hospital mortuary. This will usually be the responsibility of the funeral director. Most funeral directors

28

operate a 24-hour emergency service. However, there is no need to inform the director of a hospital death until the morning after death. If cremation is involved, the necessary forms will be filled in at the hospital. The body cannot be removed until this is done. There will be a charge for filling in the forms.

Carrying out a post mortem in a hospital

A hospital will sometimes wish to carry out a post mortem, not involving the coroner. This cannot be carried out without the permission of the next of kin. In cases where a coroner is involved permission is not required. If a coroner orders a post mortem then this is legally required and cannot be prevented. Results are not automatically given to relatives and a request for these may have to be made. The procedure for registering a death is the same as for a death outside a hospital. The registration however, must be within the district where the hospital is situated. Where there are no relatives or others to meet the cost of the funeral then the health authority has the power to do so. There are usually arrangements with local funeral directors to provide a simple funeral for the deceased.

The donation of organs for transplantation

Organ transplants help to save the lives of several thousand people per year and some thought needs to be given as to the possibility of donating organs from the dead person. Organs must be removed as soon as possible after death to prevent deterioration, which renders them useless.

No organ can be removed for transplantation until a person is declared brain dead, known as "stem" death. In order to determine brain stem death a number of stringent tests are carried out, the criteria of which are laid down by the Royal College of Surgeons.

A patient must be under 75 years of age for their major organs to be suitable for transplantation. The patient must be HIV negative and free from major infection. He or she must be of a compatible blood group to the planned recipient of the organs.

Organs that can be transplanted

Essentially, the organs intended for transplant must be in good order. For example, the lungs of a heavy smoker would be unsuitable. The following are the most commonly used for transplantation:

(overleaf)

Heart

Heart transplants are considered for those patients with severe cardiac failure who are considered unsuitable for heart surgery.

Kidney

Kidneys are viable for around 48 hours following retrieval from the donor.

Liver

Liver transplants are required for patients with congenital malformation of the liver, hepatic failure, chronic liver disease, some cases of cancer and inborn metabolic errors.

Heart and lung

This particular operation is carried out for people with an advanced primary lung disease, or a condition leading to this, or lung disease arising as a result of cardiac problems.

The pancreas

Pancreas transplants are used for patients with type 1 diabetes. This operation may be solely a pancreas transplant or can be done together with the kidneys.

Lungs

One or both lungs can be transplanted.

Cornea

Damage to the cornea is a major cause of blindness. Cornea grafting is one major solution to blindness. There is no age limit for corneal donation and corneas can be removed up to 24 hours after the heart has stopped beating. Relatives of patients not dying in a hospital who want to carry out their wishes should first of all consult the donors GP or the ophthalmic department of the local hospital.

Heart valves

These can be transplanted following removal from a donor up to 72 hours after death. There are other parts of the body, which can be transplanted including the skin, bone, connective tissue, major blood vessels, fettle cells and bone marrow. When deciding whether or not to donate organs, religious and other cultural considerations will play a significant part. For Christians, organ donation is considered acceptable to Roman Catholics and Protestants. Christian Scientists, on the other hand, object to all forms of transplants. Buddhists do not object neither does the Jewish faith, with the exception of some orthodox Jews. Mormons have no objection neither do Hindu and Sikh. Muslims tend towards prohibition of organ transplants.

The National Health Service Organ Donor Register

This register is a computer data base set up at the UK Transplant Support Service Authority (UKTSSA). All transplant coordinators have access to the register, and it can be checked each time a donor becomes available. Although relatives of donors are still asked for their permission to donate, the fact that details are on the register and there is a donor card carried, the decision is made easier by inclusion on the register.

Any driving licence issued after 1993 may be marked on the back indicating willingness to donate organs. Anyone wishing to be entered onto the register can do so by post or using a form available from doctor's surgeries, chemists, libraries and other public places.

Donation of a body for medical uses

Some people wish their body to used for medical education or research after death. If this was the wish of the deceased then the next of kin or the executor should contact HM Inspector of Anatomy for details of the relevant anatomy school. This should be done immediately after death. Offering a body may not lead to it being accepted due to too many offers or the nature of the death or whether the coroner is involved or how far away the body is.

Donation of the brain for medical research

Brain donation is a separate issue altogether from Organ donation and cannot be included on the NHS register. The Parkinson' Disease Society Brain Research Centre, which is part of the Institute of Neurology at the University College of London must be instructed to the effect that the donor wishes to donate the brain and potential donors must inform the society in advance or leave clear instructions that this should be done in the event of their death.

It will be the responsibility of the medical school to make arrangements and pay for the funeral. The school will make arrangements for a simple funeral unless the relatives indicate otherwise.

Registration in Scotland

New arrangements for the certification and registration of deaths in Scotland were introduced on **13 May 2015**. This included the establishment of an independent review service run by Healthcare

Improvement Scotland. Information on all aspects of the Death Certification Review Service is available on the Healthcare Improvement Scotland website One of the main changes is the establishment of the Death Certification Review Service which is run by Healthcare Improvement Scotland. The review service checks on the accuracy of a sample of Medical Certificates of Cause of Death (MCCDs). An MCCD is the form a doctor completes when someone has died. The Scottish Government booklet "What to do after a death in Scotland" is available on the Scottish Government website, gives practical advice for bereaved people and is widely available in registration offices. You can also get a copy by telephoning 0131 244 2193.

In Scotland the medical certificate of the cause of death is very similar to that in England. The obligation to give a certificate rests on the doctor who attended the dead person during their last illness. If there was no certificate in attendance then any doctor can issue a certificate. In most cases the certificate is given to a relative who will then send or give it to the Registrar of Deaths in their area. If a medical certificate of cause of death cannot be given, the registrar can register the death but must report the matter to the Procurator Fiscal.

There are no coroners as such in Scotland and the duties of a coroner are carried out by a Procurator fiscal. This particular person is a law officer and comes under the jurisdiction of the Lord Advocate. The key functions of the procurator fiscal includes responsibility for the investigation of all unexpected deaths including those under suspicious circumstances. If he or she is satisfied with the doctor's medical certificate and any police evidence then no further action will usually be taken. If there is doubt then a medical surgeon will be asked to report. In most cases, a post mortem is not carried out and the doctor certifies the cause of death after an external examination.

In those situations where a post mortem is deemed necessary then permission is sought from the sheriff. Where there is a possibility of criminal proceedings connected to the death then two surgeons will usually carry out the post mortem.

Death whilst in legal custody or at work must be the subject of a public enquiry which will take the place of an inquest in England. If the death is by natural causes, then there may not be a public enquiry. A public enquiry is held before the sheriff in the local sheriff court. The procurator fiscal examines the witnesses but it is the sheriff who determines the cause of death. When the enquiry

36

is completed the procurator fiscal notifies the result of the findings to the registrar general. If the death has not already been registered then the registrar general lets the local registrar in the district in which the death occurred know of the death. In Scotland the law requires that every death must be registered within eight days of death. The person qualified to act as an informant is any relative of the dead person, any person present at the death, the deceased executor or other representative, the occupier of the premises where the death took place, or any person having knowledge of the particulars to be registered.

The death may be registered in the office for the district in which the death occurred or in the office in the district where the deceased had resided before his or her death. The death of anyone visiting Scotland must be registered where the death took place.

Registering a stillbirth

A stillbirth in Scotland must be registered within 21 days. A doctor or midwife will usually issue a certificate or the person informing can fill in a form 7, issued by the local registrar. In all cases of doubt, the Procurator Fiscal will get involved. If the body is to be cremated then a certificate of stillbirth must be given by the doctor who was present at the confinement.

Death Certificates

As is the practice in England, the Registrar will issue free of charge a certificate of registration of death which can be used for National Insurance purposes. All other death certificates carry a fee. A list of fees for the various functions carried out by the registrar can be obtained from any registrar's office, as in England.

When someone dies abroad

When someone dies abroad, the death may seem more distressing because of the complications of being away from home and dealing with strangers, but you can get help from the British authorities in the UK and overseas.

Finding out about the death-If a close friend or relative dies while you are in the UK

If the death has been reported to the British Consulate in the country where the person died, they will ask the UK police to inform the next of kin. If you hear of the death from someone else, for example a tour operator, you should contact the Foreign and Commonwealth Office (FCO) on 020 7008 1500 (open 24 hours). Consular staff in London will keep in touch with the family and the Consulate abroad until burial or cremation overseas or until the deceased has been brought back to the UK.

They will also tell the British Consul of your wishes for the funeral and take details of who will be responsible for paying the costs involved, such as bringing the body back to the UK.

If the person dies while you are abroad with them

The British Consul will support you by offering practical advice and help with funeral arrangements and other formalities such as inquests. If the person died while on a package holiday, the tour operator will be able to contact funeral directors and British Consular staff for you.

Registering the death where the person died

You will need to register the death according to local regulations and get a death certificate.

The local police, British Consul or tour guide can advise you on how to do this. You can also often register the death at the British Consulate as well. You don't have to do this, but if you do you will be given a UK Death Certificate and a record will be kept at the General Registrar's Office 'Overseas' records in the UK. You will also be able to get a copy of the Death certificate later from the General Register Office or from the British Consul in the country concerned. It is not possible to register the death with the

British authorities in Australia, Canada, New Zealand, Ireland, South Africa or Zimbabwe.

Documents that you will need to register the death

When registering the death, you should take information about yourself and the deceased including:

- Full name
- Date of birth
- Passport number
- Where and when the passport was issued
- Details of the next of kin, if you are not the closest relative

Bringing the body home

If you wish to bring the body back to the UK, British Consular staff will help by putting you in touch with the international funeral director. The body will need to be embalmed and placed in a zinc-lined coffin before it can be removed from the country. It may take some time to bring the body home, especially if a post-mortem examination is held. Before you can bring the body home you will need a certified English translation of the foreign death certificate form the country in which the person died, authorization to remove the deceased's body from the country and a certificate of embalming. The British Consul can help to arrange this documentation.

Funeral costs

If the deceased's funeral costs are covered by travel insurance, contact the insurance company straight away. They will then contact the funeral directors for you and make the necessary arrangements. If the costs are not covered then all the costs concerned, including repatriation of the body and possessions will be borne by the deceased's estate.

Arranging the funeral in the UK

You will need to take an authenticated translation of the death certificate to the register office in the area you intend to hold the funeral. The registrar will then issue a 'certificate of no liability to register'. This certificate is usually given to the funeral director to enable the funeral to go ahead. The certificate is not required if a coroner has issued a Certificate E for Cremation or an Order for Burial. If you wish to have the body cremated you will need a Cremation Order (or a form E if there was a post mortem) before you start planning the funeral.

Having a funeral abroad

You can arrange for the burial or cremation in the country where the person died. The British Consulate can give you information about this.

Deaths in disasters abroad

If the deceased has been killed in a disaster abroad, natural or otherwise, ask the Foreign and Commonwealth Office for help. They will provide support and advice. The main enquiry number is 020 7008 1500. The deceased will need to be identified and you may be asked for information about them including a physical description, name and address of the person's UK doctor or dentist. The police may also need a photograph and/or finger print samples from the deceased's house.

Going to see someone who has died

If you choose to have the person who has died looked after at the undertakers, you may well want to visit them. Spending time with someone who has died isn't everyone's choice. Visiting someone who has died gives you:

- Time to accept what has happened;
- Time to let go;

- Time to take in the fact that your world has changed;
- Time to say what you have to say;
- Time to see that person looking peaceful, not as they were when they had just died.

If you think that it is a difficult thing to do consider that people who do go to see someone after death are often the better for it. If the body has been badly injured you can still go and visit. Your funeral director may be able to make the body presentable. If not arrange for the body to be covered except, say, for a hand. Or you can arrange for the coffin to be covered.

Now read the key points from Chapter one.

Key points from Chapter One.

- On discovering a person is dead, always call a doctor
- If the doctor cannot come, you must ask for permission for a Funeral Director to remove the body
- In certain circumstances, it may be necessary to call the police if the death was in suspicious circumstances
- In the United Kingdom, every death must be recorded in the coroners office within five days
- There are different rules for Scotland
- If a doctor will not issue a death certificate then the coroners office must be informed and there will be a post mortem
- In cases where an inquest has been held, the coroner will act as the person informing death
- In the case of a stillbirth the birth and death must be registered within 42 days The rules for Scotland and Northern Ireland are different.
- A different procedure applies to hospital deaths
- The decision to donate of organs will be influenced by religious and other matters

Ch. 2

Steps after Registration

If you need to make arrangements in relation to the dead person's estate then you will need to obtain several copies of the certified death certificate. You will find that a separate certificate is needed for application for probate, for dealing with banks and insurance company's etc. Before applying for the death certificate then you should estimate how many you are likely to need.

It is important that you notify the Department of Work and Pensions and any other relevant agency about the death as you will need to make arrangements about pensions etc. There may be a number of other benefits that you can claim after death, including help with funeral costs from the social fund. The funeral director may have a stock of the appropriate forms, which you must fill in.

In addition to copies of the death certificate, the registrar will provide another certificate, known as the green certificate to say that the death is now registered and a funeral can go ahead. The funeral director cannot proceed without it. If the coroner is or has been involved in the death then a different process takes place, which will be outlined a little later on. If a registrars certificate has been issued before registration then the deceased can be buried only. If it has been issued after registration then it can be cremated. The funeral director will forward the certificate either to the cemetery authority or to the vicar of the appropriate churchyard or to the office of the local crematorium.

Copies of a death certificate can be obtained at a later date from the superintendent registrar if more than one month has elapsed, or from the registrar if still relatively soon after the date of death. Applications for certificates by post can be made to the general register office, see addresses at the rear of this book. In Northern Ireland it should be made to the Registrar General. There is a fee, again relatively minor and a stamped addressed envelope will be needed.

Scotland: Apply by telephone using the Certificate Ordering Service for post-1855 births, deaths and marriages. The telephone number is 0131 314 4411 (+44 131 314 4411) and lines are open from Monday to Friday 9:00 to 16:30 except for certain public holidays. You will need to quote credit or debit card details.

Apply to a local registrar - certificates from the Scottish records may also be obtained from local registrars of births, deaths and marriages. You can find their contact details from the Directory of Registrars in Scotland or the local authority website.

Ch. 3

Taking Decisions about a Funeral

Understandably, those closest to the deceased wish to get the funeral over with as soon as is practically possible. This is a reaction to the death and to bury a person is to disassociate from the trauma of death, or at least from the first manifestations. However, it is important in all cases to ensure that a decent burial is arranged.

In some cases, the bereaved person will have left instructions in a will concerning burial. There is no strict legal obligation to go by the wishes of the deceased however although it is usual to do so. If no instructions were left then the burial arrangements will usually be arranged by the next of kin or an executor of a will. If no next of kin can be traced and there is no executor, the hospital will accept responsibility to arrange a minimum priced funeral. Although any capable person can organise a funeral, it is usual in times such as this to enlist the help of a funeral director.

A funeral director by another name is an undertaker. As with all professions, there are associations regulating the activities of funeral directors, The National Association of Funeral Directors, The Funeral Standards Council and the National Society of Allied and Independent Funeral Directors. You should make sure that a funeral director chosen by you belongs to one of the above associations. If you choose an unregistered firm then there may be no comeback in cases of future problems. The function of the funeral director is to assume complete responsibility for organising and supplying all that is needed for a funeral and also to provide as much care as is possible for relatives at this difficult time. Some funeral directors will also offer a bereavement counseling service. It is up to the deceased's family to organise a funeral and contact a director, not the executor of an estate, although in practice the executor will take on this function if requested.

A funeral director will provide a quote for a funeral and you should be clear about this at the outset. As with all services there are varying degrees of service at different prices. Insurance can be taken out for a funeral during an individual's lifetime and there are a number of so called friendly societies who offer plans. Any scheme that you invest in, as with all savings schemes has to be regulated and in the case of funeral plans the regulatory body is the National Association of Pre-Paid Funeral Plans, address and general contact details at the back of this book.

If there is a problem with money, this should be discussed with the funeral director who can assist by encouraging you to apply for a grant from the benefits agency. Normally however, the cost of a funeral is paid for from the deceased's estate.

How to find a funeral director

You shouldn't just pick the first one you find. Call around and get at least two quotes before you choose one that's best for you. You should also consider using a local independent funeral director. They're usually cheaper than a national chain. Use these sites to find a local funeral director. Make sure you check more than one site as the prices will vary.

- Fair Funerals Campaign
- The National Association of Funeral Directors
- The Society of Allied and Independent Funeral Directors

You could also use the Funeral Choice website to compare the price of your local funeral directors. You can refine the results by changing your search area. The prices shown don't include the cremation or burial fee.

Costs of a funeral

There has been much in the news recently (2018) about the costs of funerals and how there is a move by some companies, such as Co-operative Funeral Care to enter the market with lower overall costs. One of the biggest providers of funerals, Dignity, has been forced to reconsider its prices after the Co-op cut the average cost of a funeral to £1895 in England and £1675 in Scotland. The prices include collection and preparation of the body and the services of a Hearse. However, there are other costs to consider which increases the overall cost.

The price of a funeral will consist of two elements, the fees that the director pays out on the clients behalf-doctors fees, cremation fees if appropriate, fees for the minister, burial fees, gravediggers, flowers and so on. These are the people who provide a service and must be paid. Then there is the fee charged by the funeral director, removal of the deceased, preparation and arrangements, use of the chapel of rest, the hearse and limousine and bearers and so on.

Notwithstanding the ongoing price war, the overall average cost of a funeral with a traditional burial is £4,257 and the average cost of a funeral with cremation is £3,311 (according to the Royal London National Funeral Cost Index Report 2017). This will, of course, vary depending on specific choices and circumstances.

When breaking this down, there is a usual minimum price for a funeral starting with a basic funeral for around £700 plus any disbursements, usually around £300-600 for a cremation and more for a burial due to the increase in activities necessary. As far as price goes, cremation is most certainly cheaper. The average cost is around £300 as opposed for around £400 for a burial. Fees for burials will vary according to the whereabouts of the cemetery. A Church of England Burial tends to be marginally cheaper than others but most graveyards have little burial space left, often involving a second internment in a grave. Some funeral directors will charge for a complete service, including coffin while others will make a separate charge for the choice of coffin required. Funeral director will be able to show clients a range of types of coffin. The material that a coffin is made from varies and will greatly affect the price. Basic coffins are made from chipboard laminated with plastic foil. More expensive coffins are made from solid wood, usually oak. There are other coffins, made from

53

strong cardboard. However, it is always best to closely inspect the type of coffin you intend to purchase and ask questions about its durability.

Whether you buy a coffin for a cremation or for a burial will also have some bearing on the type that you buy as weaker coffins will normally suffice for cremation. Each coffin must be fitted with a nameplate of the deceased. The plate will also usually contain the age and date of death.

Associated costs

The overall cost of a funeral will consist of the funeral directors own fees and those paid to other as disbursements. However, there may well be extra costs, which are not paid direct to the funeral director, or if paid cover anything extra such as long journeys in limousines, special services etc. Any funeral director should supply you with a breakdown of what a funeral will cost before the funeral. Funeral directors will always explain different charges and conditions in various areas so that you have an idea of costs. It may well be that you decide that you wish to eliminate certain parts of the service to keep costs down. There is a fee currently for a Church of England Services £60 (check this as it may vary) for the service and £150 for a burial in the churchyard.

These are liable to change and are for guidelines only. It is always necessary to ascertain the exact cost from the funeral director. Fees for burial in a municipal city cemetery are likely to be a lot more than this.

Obtaining help with funeral costs

If a person is on low income and is in difficulties over funeral expenses there is help from the social fund administered by the Department of Work and Pensions, although such help is subject to rigid criteria. The applicant or applicants partner must be in receipt of one or more benefits, Income support, Income based Job seekers allowance, Pension Credit, Housing Benefit, Working Tax Credit where a Disability or Severe Disability element is included or Child Tax Credit which is at a higher rate than the family element.. This applies only to the person arranging the funeral. And the person applying for the benefit must be the one arranging the funeral, the next of kin or person described as the next of kin. The benefit is means tested, and if there are savings (check amounts) these will be taken into account when assessing the grant. If there is a close relative able to pay the costs of the funeral then an award will not usually be made. More details of the benefits available can be obtained from www.gov.uk/government/organisations/department-for-work-pensions which is the Department of Work and pensions website. If money becomes available out of the deceased's estate then this will be used to pay back the funeral expenses provided by the social fund. The benefits agency form is the SF200 and the funeral director can also help with this.

The Social Fund Payment will make provision for up to £700 (2018/19) towards the funeral directors fees, which must encompass almost all the costs. In addition a cremation fee will be paid and the costs of certain doctors forms. Although other small payments are made for necessary expenses the money really only provides for a simple dignified funeral. Other extras, which may be desired, are not covered. See chapter 8 for more details of benefits available. The rules for Scotland and Northern Ireland will differ. Some local authorities provide a municipal funeral service. The cost is very much less than the average local funeral and details can be obtained from your local authority. Those relatives of a member of the armed forces who die in service may be able to receive help with funeral costs from the Ministry of Defence.

Where a person dies without relatives, or no one can be traced then the local authority where the person died, or hospital if appropriate, will arrange a simple funeral. Many hospitals maintain a funeral fund and local authorities usually have close links with funeral directors.

The burial

Anyone, whether Christian or not, whose address is within the ecclesiastical parish is, in theory at least, entitled to be buried within the parish churchyard, even if a death occurs away from the parish. Some churches have burial grounds away from the church, where parishioners have the right of burial. Ex-parishioners and non-parishioners with family graves in a parish area have a right to be buried within a particular parish. It is the local vicar or parish priest who will make the decision about burial and also how much to charge. In London, certain special rules exist, under the London local Authorities Act 2007, concerning burials.

Those who are resident within the local parish have to pay a fee to the local church for a funeral service in church and burial in a churchyard. There are fees payable for a funeral service in a church and these should be checked with the local church. These fees change on an annual basis and are decided by the church. If the church service is followed by burial in a municipal or private cemetery then the fee remains the same. There is a fee for a burial in a churchyard without having had a service beforehand. No fee is payable for the burial of a stillborn child or for the funeral or burial of an infant who died within one year of birth. If the ashes are to be buried in a churchyard following cremation there is a fee and if there is to be a further service following cremation then a fee will be payable. This fee does not apply if there is a simple service of committal. There are additional fees, such as grave diggers fees, this being up to £100. This can be more expensive if a funeral director provides the gravedigger.

A vicar will allot the site of a grave in a churchyard. The burial fee does not entitle anyone to the ownership of the grave or any rights of burial there. If you want the exclusive use of a particular plot in a graveyard, you must apply to the diocesan register to reserve a grave space. This is by the grant of a licence called a faculty. The freehold of the ground, in all circumstances belongs to the church. Normally it takes about six weeks for a faculty to be granted. A faculty must be applied for before death. It is too late after death.

Burial in cemeteries

Most cemeteries are non-denominational, and are run and managed by either a local authority or a privately owned company. Particular denominations own a few cemeteries in the U.K and burial places are restricted to members of that denomination. Some cemeteries will have a section of the ground consecrated by the Church of England, while the opening of new cemeteries is attended by a service of consecration for the whole area. The fee payable to a member of the Church of England Clergy for holding a ceremony is the same as that for a funeral service in a church. There will be no church fee.

Some cemeteries have ground dedicated to, or reserved for other specific religious groups, and a separate section of general ground. In most cemeteries any type of religious service, or non-service at all, can be held. Many cemeteries have a chapel in which non-denominational services can be held. Some cemeteries will provide the services of a chaplain for burial services on a root basis. There is usually a choice of Church of England, Free Church or Roman Catholic.

Fees for burial in a cemetery vary according to where it is and who owns it. Fees are usually displayed at the cemetery. It is necessary to make enquiries as to what the fees cover and to obtain an itemised estimate of cost. In most local authority cemeteries, a higher fee is required for those who are not resident within the area. These can be double or treble the normal fees. Cemetery fees are divided into two parts: there is a charge for purchasing the exclusive rights of burial in a particular plot and an additional charge for internment. These charges will vary considerably. Most local authority cemeteries have an application form which the executor or next of kin is required to fill in. All fees must be paid before the funeral and all documents sent. Normally, as stated this will usually be dealt with by a funeral director.

Types of grave

There are different categories of grave in a cemetery. At the one end of the scale are graves without exclusive rights of burial. The person paying for a burial has no rights to say who else may be buried in the grave. The graves are given a number, marked by a number and usually it is not allowed to put up a plaque by the grave. In a few cemeteries, for a small fee a grave space can be reserved for a specific period of time from the date of payment. After this time it reverts to the cemetery. In most cemeteries it is possible to buy the right to a specific plot for a period usually not exceeding 50 years. Obviously, this is more expensive than the other options. For a private grave, a deed of grant is given for which cemeteries make a small charge. Another type of grave is what is known as the "lawn grave" in which a person has the right to exclusive burial, but can put up a simple headstone leaving the rest of the grave as grass. This grave is easier to maintain and a lot of modern cemeteries allow lawn graves only.

Other burial places

If you want to be buried in ground other than churchyard ground then the law stipulates that such burials be registered. The deeds to land, even freehold, may impose restrictions on use and enquiries should be made to local authority Environmental Health and Planning Departments. There is the right in certain circumstances to a burial at sea which will be discussed a little later. In addition, there is what is known as "woodland burial" where plots are made available in meadowland or other woodland No burial plaque or stone is normally permitted and the emphasis is on the maintenance of a natural environment.

Cremation

The majority of funerals involve the act of cremation rather than burial. As discussed earlier, cremation cannot take place until the correct certificates have been produced and the death registered. Four statutory forms have to be completed before cremation can take place; one by the next of kin or the executor, the others by three different doctors. Forms are issued by the crematorium.

Both funeral directors and doctors normally keep a supply. The first form, form A is an application for cremation and has to be completed by the next of kin or the executor and countersigned by a householder who knows that person personally. Forms B and C are on the same piece of paper and has to be completed by the doctor who attended the deceased during the last illness.

Form C is the confirmatory medical certificate, and must be completed by a doctor who has been a medical practitioner (registered) for five years or more in the United Kingdom. Doctors must not be related to the deceased or work on the same ward if they are hospital workers. In other words, they should be independent of each other.

Form F is the fourth statutory document which has to be signed by the medical referee of the crematorium, stating that he or she is satisfied with the details on forms B and C, or the coroners certificate for cremation. The medical referee can prevent cremation taking place and can order a post mortem to take place or refer the matter to the coroner. Relatives have no right to prevent this post mortem. If they do not want it to take place then they must bury the deceased instead.

When the coroner is involved and has ordered a post mortem, he or she will issue a certificate for cremation. Forms B and C are not required. When a death is reported to the coroner, he or she must be informed at the outset if the funeral is to involve cremation, so that the appropriate certificate can be issued. This is form E and will be supplied as a pink form to the relatives so that they may register and as a yellow form to the funeral director for submission to the crematorium.

If the body of a stillborn child is to be cremated, a special medical certificate has to be issued by a doctor who was present at the birth, or who examined the body after birth. No second medical certificate is required, but the medical referee still has to complete form F. Many crematoria do not charge for the cremation of stillborn children, or infants up to the age of one year.

Fees for cremation

Fees include the charges made by the crematorium, the fees for the doctor's certificates and usually a standard fee for the minister who takes the service. An organist also needs to be paid in addition to other costs. The funeral director will usually pay all fees and charge accordingly. Crematorium fees on average are from £600 with extra fees for those who did not reside in the district of cremation. Doctors who prepare initial forms will usually charge a minimum fee which rises each year. On occasions, when death has occurred in a hospital, the hospital will wish to carry out a post mortem to improve their knowledge of the patient's condition. The consent of relatives must be given and if so, form C will not be required-providing the post mortem was carried out by a pathologist of not less than five years standing and the result known by the doctor who completed form B. Only one fee will be charged, unless the pathologist was less than five years standing, in which case another doctor must complete form C and the full fee will be charged. Most crematoria charge reduced fees for children up to school leaving age. You should check the above fees as they change subject to notice.

The majority of crematoria are run by local authorities, although private crematoria do exist. Each has its scale of fees and offers a brochure of services and fees, usually having an open day for the public, usually Sunday, as crematoria are open only from Monday to Friday, with occasional Saturdays.

Services in a crematorium

Charges for a crematorium will normally include the chapel, whether or not it is used. Chapels are non-denominational, catering for a variety of religions. Music can be chosen by the relatives. If they wish, relatives can opt for a non-religious funeral. Funeral directors can usually refer you to someone who can organise this.

Cremations and memorials

Most crematoriums will have various forms of memorial. There will be a book of remembrance in which the name of the deceased can be inscribed. Other memorials involve wall plaques, memorial flowers or rose bushes. There will usually be an extra charge for this. Some more sophisticated crematoria have extensive means of remembrance in their landscaped gardens. Again, there will be a charge for this.

Remains

Cremated remains or ashes of the deceased may be scattered in the grounds of the crematorium, taken away to be scattered elsewhere or buried in a local churchyard or cemetery. The crematorium will not usually charge a fee for scattering ashes after a funeral. However, a fee will be charged if ashes are stored and scattered later. There will usually be a fee if the ashes are to be scattered in a crematorium to the one where the funeral took place. There is a Church of England Charge for the burial of ashes in a churchyard.

This is around £123, at current prices, increasing annually. However, these prices should be checked with the relevant church. A useful leaflet concerning cremation, "Questions People ask" is available from some local crematoria.

Direct Cremation

Direct cremation is offered by some companies - where the body is collected from a mortuary during normal working hours and cremated at a convenient time. There's usually no viewing or ceremony beforehand, or a limousine for the family and mourners. And if you wish to have the ashes afterwards, make sure you request them. You usually need to collect them, but some might deliver for a charge. This then leaves you to hold a ceremony, if you wish, at a time and place of your choosing.

Costs of a direct cremation

A budget of about £1,600 is suggested. There are several companies online offering direct cremation for around £1,000. This price normally includes third party costs such as doctor's certification and crematorium fees. If you'd like to have the ashes returned to you, this can cost an extra £100. And collecting the body outside of normal working hours, or from a nursing home or residence, is about an extra £500. This brings the total cost of a direct cremation to £1,600. Costs might vary depending on location. So, shop around and check whether the company offers a reasonable price for covering your area.

If you choose to hold a ceremony afterwards, you'll need to factor in these costs as well. However, there are a variety of low cost ways to have a ceremony, such as having it at home.

How to find one a provider of direct cremations

You can do an online search for 'direct cremation' in your area. If you're in England or Wales, you could try these national providers:

- Woodland Wishes
- Simplicity Cremations
- Simplicita Cremations
- Pure Cremation
- Memoria

Or use these sites below to find a local provider.

- Fair Funerals Campaign
- The National Association of Funeral Directors
- The Society of Allied and Independent Funeral Directors

Make sure you check more than one site as they will show different results. Some might not provide direct cremations.

Events before a funeral

Most funeral directors maintain a 24-hour service. If death occurs at home or in a nursing home, two funeral directors will arrive fairly rapidly and take the body to the mortuary. It is rare for a body to remain at home between death and the funeral although is possible if requested by relatives. It is recommended that a funeral director be approached as soon as is possible after a death.

When a body is taken by a funeral director then it will lie in a chapel of rest, where the body will lie in a coffin before the funeral. Laying out of a body will almost always take place in the funeral director mortuary. Arrangements need to be made about any jewelry and also clothes, as the funeral director can supply a gown if necessary. If a person dies in hospital the body is usually taken to the hospital mortuary-although a number of hospitals normally subcontract mortuary facilities to a funeral director. When a body is removed by a funeral director it will lie until cremation papers have been completed. If a coroner has decided that a post mortem is necessary then the body will be taken to the mortuary in preparation.

When a body is kept in a chapel of rest, relatives and friends can go to see it before the funeral. Sometimes, there will be an extra charge to see the body at evenings and weekends. Some larger firms of funeral directors also have chapels for private prayer, in which a religious service can be held at the beginning of the funeral before the cortege leaves for the cemetery or crematorium.

Embalming a body

The process of embalming is intended to delay the process of decomposition of a body. The blood in a body is replaced with a preservative, normally a solution of formalin. This is similar to a blood transfusion. It is necessary to embalm a body if it is returned to a private house to await a funeral or if the funeral is to be held more than five days after a death and cannot be put into cold storage. Before a body can be embalmed, a doctor must have completed the medical certificate of the cause of death and the death registered.

When cremation is involved, forms B and C must also have been completed. If the coroner is involved then embalming cannot take place unless permission has been obtained. Embalmers are qualified and no one else other than a qualified person should be used.

The final arrangements before a funeral

The funeral director must have the registrar's disposal certificate before confirming the final arrangements. All of the functions connected with burial or cremation must have been completed and all fees paid.

The funeral director or a member of the family should ask whoever the family wishes to officiate at the service whether they can or are willing to do so, and at the allotted time or date. Services can be held in a church, churchyard, cemetery, crematorium chapel, village hall or any other suitable place. Funeral services can be held anywhere, with no particular form of licensing necessary.

Non-Church of England Funerals

Denominational burial grounds usually insist on their own form of service. For a practicing Roman Catholic it is usual for a priest to say a requiem mass in the local parish church and for the priest to take the funeral service.

With Orthodox Jews, the body should be buried as soon as possible once the disposal certificate has been issued. If a man subscribes to a synagogue burial society, he or his wife and

70

children will be buried free by the society in its cemetery. Orthodox Jews are never cremated, and embalming or bequeathing a body for medical purposes is never allowed. There are usually no flowers. The burial is simple. Reform non-orthodox Jews are not so rigid and permit cremation and flowers. If a Jew dies away from home it is the responsibility of the relatives to bring the body back at their own expense for the synagogue burial society to take over.

Non-religious services

There is no obligation to have a ceremony at a funeral. It is important to communicate this to the executor or person in charge if this is the case. If a body is to be buried in a churchyard without a religious ceremony, or by someone of another denomination, you should give at least 48 hours notice in writing. Usual fees are still applicable. If the body is to be buried in a cemetery or cremated without religious ceremony, the funeral director or local authority should be informed. If there is to be no ceremony then usually a few members will attend the funeral and there will be a few minutes silence or with some music played.

Announcements of deaths are usually made in local papers. Sometimes, the national dailies will have an announcement. The address of the deceased should never be inserted in the obituary. A lot of houses have been broken into when a funeral takes place. The press notice should stipulate requirements for the giving of money to the deceased's favorite charity and also for flowers. The time and date and other arrangements for the funeral are included, and these details should be tailored to a families requirements. When a body is buried, flowers are normally left on a grave after it has been filled in. At a crematorium there will normally be restrictions as to where flowers can be placed.

The funeral

Although it was tradition for the cortege (procession) to travel from the house to the place of the funeral it is just as common, given the prominence of the funeral director, for the funeral to begin from the premises of the funeral director. If the funeral director provides cars for the relatives and friends of the deceased then he or she will organise and marshal the event and arrange departure.

The funeral director should have discussed all the details of the funeral with the family beforehand, and also arrange where people are to be taken after the funeral and also take care of other last minute arrangements. The funeral director may walk in front of the hearse as it leaves the deceased's house, and as it approaches the church or crematorium. This is both a mark of respect to the deceased and also a practical arrangement as he can direct the traffic. The coffin will be usually carried into the church or crematorium on the shoulders (or by handles on the coffin) of the funeral directors staff. Sometimes members of the family act as bearers. Occasionally, at the more formal funeral, pall-bearers walk alongside the coffin.

The burial

If a burial is preceded by a service in church, the coffin is taken into the church by the bearers and placed in front of the altar. In Roman Catholic churches the coffin is taken into the church before the funeral and remains there until the funeral takes place. After the service the bearers will take the coffin from the church to the churchyard or cemetery. If a burial is not preceded by a church service then the coffin is taken directly from the hearse to the cemetery. The coffin is lowered into the grave while the words of committal are said. A register of burial in the parish area is kept by the church. Copies can be obtained for a small fee.

When someone is buried in a Church of England churchyard, the family is responsible for the grave. Municipal and private cemeteries will employ grounds men to look after the common

73

parts and also graves. Cemeteries often stipulate the provision of a simple grave in order to keep costs of maintenance down. A lot of churches have restrictions on the type of headstones and memorials used and it will be necessary to check with the church first before making any decisions.

Cremation

Traditionally, the funeral service prior to cremation was held in church, with the congregation travelling to the crematorium for a brief committal afterwards. It is an increasing practice for funeral services to be held entirely in a crematorium chapel. When the words of committal are spoken, the coffin passes out of site although some mourners prefer the coffin to remain until the last mourner has left the chapel.

During the funeral service, the funeral directors staff will take flowers from the hearse and place them in the floral display area. The funeral director will take appropriate flowers to a hospital or nursing homes after the mourners have left. When the coffin is out of site it is taken to the committal room to await cremation. When the cremation process is complete the ashes are refined separately and placed in containers.

In the process of making arrangements for the cremation, the next of kin or executors of the deceased person's estate can ask to be present when the coffin is placed in the cremator. This is especially relevant for Hindu funerals where traditionally the next of kin would light the funeral pyre. Usually, only two people are allowed. Each crematorium will keep a register of cremations and again a copy can be obtained for a small fee. When making arrangements for a funeral, clients are asked what they would like to do with the ashes. While most ashes are scattered or buried in the crematorium grounds they can also be removed by next of kin to be scattered or buried elsewhere. When ashes are removed, the crematorium will normally provide a certificate confirming that the cremation has taken place. If ashes are to be scattered in the grounds of a different crematorium, there will be a fee of up to £30. There is no law regulating the disposal of ashes, they can be scattered anywhere, with consent from owners etc.

Burial in Scotland

In Scotland it is possible to purchase the exclusive rights to burial in a cemetery or churchyard (Kirkyard) plot. A grave is called a lair. Kirkyards are administered by the local district or islands council. Regulations and procedures for cremation are the same as in England and Wales.

Arranging a funeral without a funeral director

It is possible to arrange a funeral without using a funeral director. Most people will want a funeral director to take care of matters after death, due to grief and the wish to arrange matters quickly. However, some people prefer to arrange their own funeral.

If the coroner is not involved, a doctor's certificate as to the cause of death must be obtained and the death registered. The appropriate papers must be obtained and sent to the cemetery or crematorium with a fee. A date and time for the funeral must be arranged. A minister should be approached if they are to conduct the funeral. A coffin must be obtained along with the means of conveying the coffin to the funeral. If a burial is taking place a gravedigger must be hired

With cremation, the papers as outlined in this book must be obtained and a coffin and crematoria arrangements made. Coffins can be purchased from funeral supermarkets or from a funeral director. It is always highly advisable to purchase a coffin and not attempt to make one yourself. Biodegradable coffins can also be purchased for a fairly low price. These are normally made of cardboard. Details can be obtained from the natural death centre, address at the back of this book.

It is possible to arrange for a burial to take place on your own land-in a garden or a field. Planning permission is not necessary. However, there are other restrictions, one being the level of the water table and if this is likely to be affected. Other difficulties can arise, one being if a family or person decides to move house. A Home Office Licence is required to exhume a body.

As stated, although it is possible to carry out a funeral yourself, without a funeral director, it is not a common occurrence because of the amount of work involved. Many people decide to leave this to a funeral director. At this point, it is worth outlining the practice of 'Green Funerals' as this is the choice of people who are either into environmentally friendly funerals or natural burials, where communing with nature is paramount.

Green funerals

A green funeral is an ethical choice and one which seeks not to harm the environment. It is also, for some, an aesthetic choice, which may appeal to those who have no particular environmental interests but rejects the traditional stuffy funeral in favour of an out doors, homespun, back to nature feel. It prefers an unspoilt landscape to that of a regimented ceremony.

An Real Green funeral

The elements of a real green funeral are as follows:

- Rejection of cremation
- Opts for burial in a site serving a conservation purpose
- Creates a site which is not visually definable as a burial ground
- Reviles embalming
- Requires a coffin or shroud locally made from natural sustainable material
- Buries the body at a depth where it can decompose aerobically
- Rejects bought flowers, prefers garden flowers (if any)
- Forbids demarcation of the grave
- Forbids marking or personalizing of the grave with any sort of permanent memorial
- Forbids tending of the grave
- Discourages visits to the grave unless on foot or bike.

A real green funeral leaves no trace behind. However, there are at present very few burial sites that meet the above criteria. Most people who favour a natural burial want their decomposed body to nourish the plants and soil around it. Natural burial is a very personal form of recycling. Many like the idea of a tree planted on top of them. In a local authority cemetery, by law, no part of a coffin must be less than three feet below the surface except where soil conditions allow, in which case two feet will do. This is too deep to ensure truly vibrant aerobic decomposition. This law does not apply to private burial grounds. However, the Ministry of Justice is urging compliance. Almost all natural burial grounds bury bodies at a depth where decomposition will be cold, slow and mostly anaerobic.

There are pluses and minuses when considering a green/natural burial as opposed to a conventional funeral. The Association of Natural Burial Grounds lists all green grounds in the UK. This site can also point the way to organizations that can give you more advice. Details can be found at the Natural Death Centre below.

The Natural Death centre

The Natural Death Centre is a charity which campaigns for a change in social attitudes to death and dying. The philosophy of the NDC grew out of that of the natural childbirth movement. The NDC believes that tasking control; and keeping interventions by strangers to a minimum improves the quality of dying for the dying person and its impact on his or her carers. In the matter of caring for the dead it believes that taking control is therapeutic.

The NDC encourages and supports those who want to arrange environmentally friendly and inexpensive funerals, and it is behind the Association of Natural Burial Grounds –anbg.co.uk.

A hands on approach to dealing with the dying and the dead strongly appeals to people of all sorts who know their own minds and like to do things their own way. The NDC publishes The Natural Death Handbook, which is full of practical advice and personal stories. It operates a telephone helpline and offers free advice on all aspects of natural death and funerals.

Contact the NDC: naturaldeath.org, phone 01962 712 690

Now read the key points from chapter three.

Key points from Chapter three

- In some cases the deceased person will have left instructions concerning his/her funeral. If no instructions were left the funeral will usually be arranged by the next of kin or the executor of the estate. If no next of kin can be traced and there is no executor then the hospital (if appropriate) will accept responsibility to arrange a minimum price funeral.

- A funeral director will usually carry out all the arrangements concerning the funeral

- A funeral will be more expensive than a cremation

- The Department of Work and Pensions can provide advice about help towards funeral for those on low incomes

- In London, under the London Local Authorities Act 2007, Councils can disturb human remains that have been buried for at least 75 years to deepen graves and allow more burials.

- Green funerals are the choice of people who want a more natural funeral.

Ch. 4

Different Funerals

As Great Britain is a multi-racial society, obviously not all funeral and burials are Christian burials. Some space has to be given in a book like this to cover other funerals as they relate to different beliefs.

Muslim funerals

There are specific codes governing Muslim funerals. Normally, Muslims will appoint one person to represent them in making arrangements for funerals. Muslims are always buried and never cremated. There is usually no coffin and the body is wrapped in a white sheet and buried within 24 hours of death in an unmarked grave, which must be raised up to 12 inches from the ground and can never be sat or walked upon.

Because of differences between the British tradition and Muslim requirements, one key difference being that a coffin is required in British cemeteries, special areas are sometimes designated by churches and other cemeteries. Because of the need to bury quickly, any requests for post mortem or organ donation are usually refused, although a post mortem will be necessary in the cases of suspicious deaths.

Muslims believe that the soul remains in the body sometime after death, and that the body remains conscious of pain. Bodies are therefore handled with care. Non-Muslims never handle bodies. Embalming is only usually allowed if a body is travelling over a long distance. The family will usually lay out a body and will place a head so that it is facing Mecca. Muslims must be buried facing Mecca. The family will normally perform all rites and blessings, together with the imam, the spiritual leader of the local mosque.

Hindu funerals

There are many Hindu deities, the three main being Brahma, the creator, Vishnu, the Preserver and Shiva, the Destroyer. Hindu belief in reincarnation means that most individuals face death in the hope of achieving a better life next time. Death is therefore relatively insignificant by comparison. Hindus are always cremated and never buried. Most Hindus bring their dead into a chapel of rest and candles are lit. There are not normally objections to the body being handled by non-Hindu, although

83

there can be many variations on the theme because of the diversity of the religion. The Asian Funeral Service arranges Hindu funerals and organises repatriation for those who require a funeral by the Ganges.

Sikh funerals

Sikhism has a lot in common with Hinduism but there is a strong emphasis on militarism. There are five symbols of faith important to the Sikh. The Kesh is the uncut hair, which, for men, is always turbaned. The Kangha is a ritual comb, which keeps the hair in place and is never removed. The Kara is a steel bracelet worn on the right wrist. The Kirpan is a small symbolic dagger. The Kaccha are ceremonial undergarments, which are never completely removed even when bathing.

Sikhs are always cremated and never buried. The family will always insist that their dead are buried with all five K symbols.

After a death, men are dressed in a white cotton shroud and turban, older women in white and young women in red. Cremation will usually take place within 24 hours. The coffin will usually be taken home before cremation for last respects to be paid. The oldest son will press the crematoria button or see the coffin into the cremator. Ashes are scattered in a river or in the sea or taken back for scattering in the Punjab in India.

Buddhist funerals-Buddhist beliefs about death

Buddhists acknowledge death as a part of the cycle of reincarnation known as samsāra. In samsāra, a Buddhist's actions in life will affect future incarnations. Although widely accepted among Buddhists, this belief may differ slightly according to the type of Buddhism. Buddhists aspire to leave the cycle of samsāra by freeing themselves from all desires and notions of self to attain enlightenment and reach a state of nirvana.

Buddhist cremation

Many Buddhists prefer cremation to burial. Traditionally, Buddhist cremation may take place on an open air pyre, but as this is prohibited in the UK, most Buddhists choose a cremation service at a local crematorium. The cremation ashes may be scattered, buried or kept at home in an urn.

In some Buddhist cultures, such as in Japan, the family may want to watch the cremation process take place. This may be possible at your local crematorium – ask your funeral director if this can be arranged. However, burial is not unheard of in Buddhist funerals.

Some Buddhists may opt for a woodland burial, as an environmentally-friendly way to return to the earth.

Buddhist funeral traditions

Organ and body donation for transplant and research purposes are acceptable within Buddhism. Embalming is generally not encouraged, unless it is completely necessary or the individual expressed a wish to be embalmed.

Buddhist funeral services

Normally Buddhist funerals are simple and dignified, and take place at a Buddhist monastery or at a family home. The number of mourners expected can vary, often depending on the size of the venue.

There is no prescribed procedure that Buddhist funerals follow, so the funeral service may occur before cremation, after cremation or before burial. Depending on the arrangements, there may be an open coffin at the funeral service.

On arrival, mourners may be see an altar decorated with an image of the person who has died, an image of Buddha, flowers, incense, candles and fruits. Mourners often present the bereaved with flowers, usually placed alongside their loved one or the decorated altar. Once all the mourners have paid their respects, monks and other members of the Buddhist community will read sermons and deliver eulogies. Chanting by monks regularly features in Buddhist funeral services, although the recordings of chants are sometimes played on these occasions instead. Non-religious rites may be performed alongside those of Buddhism, as long as they do not conflict with Buddhist funeral rites and beliefs.

After a Buddhist funeral

Buddhism is a very diverse religion, existing in many different cultures. Whether or not there is a reception after the funeral may depend on the traditions of the family. Usually, if there is a reception, mourners will be invited to attend to pay their respects. Traditionally, Buddhist memorial services are held on the 3rd, 7th, 49th and 100th day after death. These dates, however, can be changed at the family's discretion.

Jewish funerals

Orthodox Jews are very strict when it comes to funerals while more progressive Jews have differing attitudes. When a Jewish person dies, the body is traditionally left for eight minutes while a feather is placed in the mouth or nostrils to detect signs of breathing. Eyes and mouth are then closed by the eldest son, or the nearest relative. Many Jews appoint "watchers" this being a person or people who will stay with the body day or night until the funeral, praying and reciting.

The dead are buried as soon as possible. Cremation is not accepted by the Orthodox Jew. Orthodox Rabbis will sometimes permit the burial of cremated remains in a full size coffin, and say Kaddish (prayer) for the deceased. Jewish funerals are usually arranged by a Jewish funeral agency. Otherwise, the local Jewish community will arrange a contract with a gentile Funeral Director, but under strict Rabbinical control. The Raphael Jewish Counseling Service offers support to those who have lost another raphaeljewishcounselling.org. 0800 234 6236.

Cult funerals

There are an enormous number of different Christian cults in the U.K., including Mormons and Jehovah's Witnesses, Christian Scientists, Scientologists, Moonies and the Children of God. For most there is little or no deviation from orthodox Christian practice. Some groups became prominent in the 1960's, such as Hare Krishna and will normally adopt Hindu practices.

Now read the key points from chapter four.

Key points from chapter four

■ Great Britain is a multi-racial society and it is important that those who reside here show sensitivity to the customs of other cultures as they apply to groups in the U.K.

■ There are specific codes governing Muslim funerals. Normally, Muslims will appoint one person to represent them in making arrangements for funerals.

■ Hindus are always cremated and never buried.

■ Sikhism has a lot in common with Hinduism but there is a strong emphasis on militarism.

■ Buddhists acknowledge death as a part of the cycle of reincarnation known as samsāra. In samsāra, a Buddhist's actions in life will affect future incarnations.

■ When a Jewish person dies, the body is traditionally left for eight minutes while a feather is placed in the mouth or nostrils to detect signs of breathing. Eyes and mouth are then closed by the eldest son, or the nearest relative.

Ch. 5

After a Funeral is Over

Traditional funerals

When a funeral service is finished, there is usually a gathering of family and friends at the house of the deceased, or at a venue organized by relatives. The organising of this event is important as mourners need to be clearly informed about what has been arranged and where it is being held.

The funeral director (If used depending on the funeral) will submit an account, which is usually very detailed and will require payment within a reasonable amount of time. If the money is from the estate, there should be no problem arranging for the release of the funds to pay for a funeral. Legally, payment of the funeral bill is the first claim on the estate of the deceased, taking priority over income tax and any other claims.

Memorials

Relatives of the deceased often want to place a memorial tablet or headstone in a churchyard or cemetery where the person is buried. There are normally restrictions on the size of the memorial and full details of the restrictions can be obtained from the burial ground. The funeral director or monumental mason will normally apply to the church or cemetery authorities for permission to erect a memorial. After a burial, several months should be allowed for settlement before any memorial is erected or replaced. Time and consideration should be given to a memorial, and names of Burial Authorities. The cost of memorial will vary enormously, depending on what has been purchased and a written estimate should be obtained before any order is given.

After cremation

About one week after cremation has taken place, the crematorium will usually send a brochure to the next of kin explaining what kinds of memorials are available. These are all optional and are not covered by the fees paid for the cremation.

The most popular means of memorial at the cremation is the book of remembrance. Hand lettered inscriptions in the book usually consist of the name, date of death, and a short epitaph. The charge depends on the length of entry. The crematorium displays the book, open at the right page, on the anniversary of the funeral.

The crematoria will provide a list of charges on request. Some crematoria have a colonnade of niches for ashes called a columbarium. The ashes are either walled in by a plaque or left in an urn by the niche. Charges for this are high, where space can be found. In addition to the above, some crematoria have memorial trees, or rose bushes. These are usually arranged in beds, where the memorial bush is chosen by the family, the ashes are scattered around it, and a small plaque placed nearby. Costs vary and can be provided by the crematoria in question.

Ashes generally

Once a cremation is over, if you want you can get the ashes back. There are a number of things that you can do with the ashes. You can bury them in your local cemetery or in a natural burial ground. You can scatter them. You can divide them up amongst members of the family. You can get the crematorium to scatter them. There are many things that can be done with the ashes. Here are a few suggestions :

- Keep the ashes in an urn, this is a very common way of dealing with the ashes
- Mix them in clay or some other material and make something with them

- Scatter them from a hot air balloon or aircraft

- Scatter them at sea

- Have them turned into a diamond-go to phoenix-diamonds.com

- Have them mixed with glass and made into an ornament or pendant. Go to ashesintoglass.co.uk

- Keep them in a locket, ring or pendant. Go to urns-coffins-caskets.co.uk

- Have them made into a firework display. Go to heavensabovefireworks.com

- Fire them into space. Go to heavensabovefireworks.com

These are just a few options for you to think about.

Charitable donations

An increasing number of people will request that family and friends make a charitable donation to a nominated charity in memory of the deceased and will regard this as a fitting memorial for the person concerned. Usually, the funeral director will arrange to collect and forward donations and will not charge for this service.

Ch. 6

The Estate of the Deceased-Applying for Probate-England and Wales, Scotland and Northern Ireland

---

England and Wales

Probate simply means that the executor's powers to administer the estate of a dead person have been officially confirmed. A document called a "Grant of Representation" is given which enables those administering the estate to gain access to all relevant information, financial or otherwise concerning the person's estate.

Although anyone charged under a will to act on behalf of the dead persons estate has automatic authority to represent, there are certain cases where evidence of probate is required. If no will exists or no executors have been appointed, then it will be necessary to obtain "letters of administration" which involves a similar procedure. Under common law, probate has a number of objectives.

These are: (overleaf)

- To safeguard creditors of the deceased
- To ensure reasonable provision is made for the deceased's dependants
- To distribute the balance of the estate in accordance with the intentions of the person whose will it is.

One of the key factors affecting the need to obtain probate is how much money is involved under the terms of a will. Where the sums involved are relatively small then financial institutions and other organisations will not normally want to see evidence of probate. However, it should be remembered that no one is obliged to release anything relating to a dead person's estate unless letters of administration or documents of probate can be shown. Those responsible for administering the estate must find out from the organisations concerned what the necessary procedure is.

Applying for probate

Where a will is in existence and executors have been appointed then any one of the named people can make the application. Where a will is in existence but no executors have been appointed, then the person who benefits from the whole estate should make the application. This would be the case where any known executor cannot or will not apply for probate. Where there is no will in existence then the next of kin can apply for probate. There is an order of priority relating to the application:

- The surviving spouse
- A child of the deceased
- A parent of the deceased
- A brother or sister of the deceased
- Another relative of the deceased

The person applying for probate must be over eighteen. Children includes any that are illegitimate. If a child dies before the deceased then one of his or her children can apply for probate.

Making the application

This can be done through any probate registry or office. There is usually one in every main town and any office in any area will accept the application. If you are writing then you should always address your correspondence to a registry and not an office.

What needs to be done next?

The next of kin should register the death with the Register of Births and Deaths. A death certificate will be supplied and copies of the death certificate obtained, which will need to be included to various institutions and organisations. A copy of the will has to be obtained. The whereabouts should be known to the executors. The executor should then take a copy of the will in case the original is lost. The executor will need to obtain full details of the dead person's estate, including all property and other items together with a current valuation. It is possible that on many of the less substantial items a personal valuation can be made. It should however, be as accurate as possible.

In the case of any bank accounts a letter should be sent by the executor to the bank manager, stating that he/she is the executor and giving full details of the death. Details should be requested concerning the amount of money in the dead person's account(s) together with any other details of valuables lodged with the bank. The bank manager may be able to pass on information concerning holdings in stocks and shares. If share certificates are held then a valuation of the shares at time of death should be requested.

In the case of insurance policies, the same procedure should be followed. A letter should be sent to the insurance company requesting details of policies and amounts owed or payable. In the case of National Savings Certificates the executor should write to the Savings Certificate Office in Durham and ask for a list of all certificates held, date of issue and current value. In the case of Premium Bonds a letter should be sent to National Savings and Investments, Glasgow G58 1SB giving name and date of death. Premium Bonds remain in the draw for 12 months after death, so they can be left invested for that time or cashed in when probate has been obtained. Form SB4 (obtained from any post office) is used to inform of death and obtain repayment of most government bonds.

In the case of property, whatever valuation is put on a property HM Revenues and Customs can always insist on its own valuation. If there is a mortgage, the executor should write to the mortgagee asking for the amount outstanding at the time of death. The above procedure should be followed when writing to any one or an organisation, such as a pension fund, requesting details of monies owed to the dead person.

Debts owed by the person

The executor will need to compile a list of debts owed by the dead person as these will need to be paid out of the estate. These debts will include all money owed, loans, overdrafts, bills and other liabilities. If there is any doubt about the extent of the debts then the executor can advertise in the London Gazette and any newspaper, which circulates in the area where the estate is situated. Efforts also have to be made to locate creditors outside of advertising. The advert will tell creditors that they have to claim by a certain date after which the estate will be administered having obtained probate. Funeral expenses should be quantified and a letter should be sent to HMRC to determine the income tax position of the dead person. The executor obtains the application form, decide where he or she wishes to be interviewed, sends the completed form together with the death certificate and the original will to the Probate Registry and then attend for an interview.

The forms

The forms consist of the following:

Form PR1-Probate Application form

Form IHT 205 short form where inheritance tax not due

Form IHT 200 long form where tax due

There will be instructions on application as to how to fill these forms in. It may be possible for an interview to take place on the same day as the forms are received by the appropriate office. The forms can be delivered either personally or by post.

The interview

The interview is to iron out any problems with the application and to get the executor to swear or affirm before the Probate Officer that the information in the forms is true (to the best of knowledge). The taxation form for inheritance purposes has to be signed so that it can be returned to HMRC for assessment. Probate fees have to be paid at the interview. These are worked out on the value of the net estate. A list of current fees can be obtained from any Probate Office. After the interview the Probate Registry will send the account of the estate to the capital taxes office for an assessment of any inheritance tax payable. Once the Probate Registry has received an assessment then this will be sent to the executor who should then make arrangements for payment.

The tax should be paid before Probate is granted or letters of administration are given. It must be paid within six months of the date of death. After a few weeks, the executor will receive grant of Probate. This is simply a sheet of paper which details that the dead person, of a particular address died on a particular day and that the executor has been granted the administration of the estate. The gross and net value at a specific date are stated. Attached is the probate copy of the will. The executor receives the original death certificate. All probate documents become public property which are open for inspection by the public. Further copies of probate documents can be obtained for a fee.

Dealing With a Deceased's Estate in Scotland

Applying for confirmation

When dealing with a deceased's estate in Scotland, you may have been told that you need to obtain 'confirmation' before any money and other property, belonging to the deceased, can be released. It is often a bank, building society or insurance company that will ask for this.

'Confirmation' is a legal document from the court giving the executor(s) authority to uplift any money or other property belonging to a deceased person from the holder (such as the bank), and to administer and distribute it according to law. An application is lodged with the sheriff court to commence the process. This is only one part of the process in dealing with a deceased's estate, and is the part that the court is involved in. You will find some useful information on other parts of the process in

102

the document What to do after a death in Scotland......practical advice for times of bereavement, produced by the Scottish Government.

When applying for confirmation, an executor must provide a list of all the deceased's property at the time of death. The list - called an inventory - might include money, houses, land and shares. Confirmation is possible only if the inventory includes at least one item of money or other property in Scotland.

Small Estate or Large Estate

There are two types of confirmation, for **small estates** and for **large estates**. A 'small estate' is an estate where the total value of the deceased's money and property is £36000 or less. A 'large estate' is an estate where the total value is above this. In calculating the total value, you should not deduct any debts, such as funeral expenses, gas or electricity bills, balance of mortgage, owed by the deceased. The values of bank accounts must also include interest to date of death.

The procedure, forms and fees are different depending on what type of estate the application relates to. If the estate is a small estate, then the sheriff clerk will be able to help you prepare the 'inventory', and you can contact your local sheriff court to arrange an appointment.

If the estate is a large estate, we would recommend seeking legal advice. The Law Society of Scotland www.lawsot.org can provide contact details for solicitors in your area.

Presence of a will

The procedures are also different depending on whether or not the deceased left a will. If they did not leave a will, you might hear the estate being referred to as 'intestate'; if they did leave a will, you might hear the estate being referred to as 'testate'. If there was a will left and it complies with all of the legal requirements in Scotland, then the information noted above in relation to small and large estates will apply. If they did not leave a will, then you may have to get a bond of caution before you apply for confirmation of the estate, further information on this can be received from the sheriff clerk. If it is a large estate, and there is no will, there is an additional step in the procedure. You would need to apply to be appointed executor, using the dative petition procedure. We would advise seeking legal advice in relation to this.

Applications after confirmation has been issued:

- where the original executor has died or has become incapacitated without fully administering the estate of the deceased (Ad non executa); or

- where additional estate is discovered or where estate has been wrongly valued in the original confirmation and the principal executors appointed will not, or cannot act (*Ad omissa*).

The form to be used is Form X-1 Confirmation ad non executa / ad omissa. An application can also be made to court where an asset was not included in the original inventory. To do this, you would need to complete a corrective inventory and the form to be used is Form C4(S). Further information can be accessed on the HMRC website.

How much will it cost?

The fees for applying for confirmation will depend on the value of the estate and the number of certificates you need to provide for different banks, insurance companies etc. to allow them to release the funds.

You should note that these fees do not include any fees you may need to pay if you have instructed a solicitor to help you. The solicitor can give you information on these costs.

You cannot apply for fee exemption when applying for confirmation unless the estate of the deceased person is exempt from inheritance tax by virtue of:

- section 153A (death of emergency service personnel etc.),
- section 154 (death in active service etc.), or
- section 155A (death of constables and service personnel targeted because of their status)

of the Inheritance Tax Act 1984 in which case there is no fee in respect of the inventory of that estate. However, fees for certificates, copies, etc. remain payable in these circumstances.

Dealing with a deceased's estate Northern Ireland

A grant in Northern Ireland is almost always needed when the person who died leaves one or more of the following:

- £10,000 or more
- stocks or shares
- certain insurance policies

- property or land held in their own name or as 'tenants in common'

In most cases above, the bank or relevant institution will need to see the grant before transferring control of the assets. However if the estate is small some organisations, such as insurance companies and building societies, may choose to release the money to you.

You may not need a grant if the deceased:

- left less than £10,000
- owned everything jointly with someone else and everything passes automatically to the surviving joint owner

To find out if the assets can be obtained without a grant, the executor or administrator would need to write to each institution informing them of the death and enclosing a photocopy of the death certificate and will if there is one.

Inheritance tax

You'll need to deal with inheritance tax before you can apply for probate. The tax form you need to complete depends on if you expect inheritance tax to be due on the estate. Inheritance tax is paid if a person's estate (their property, money and possessions) is worth more than £325,000 when they die. You can ask a solicitor to help you or you can do it yourself.

Inheritance tax due	Inheritance tax form(s) required
Yes	Inheritance Tax Account Form IHT400 Probate summary Form IHT421
No	Return of Estate Information Form IHT205

There are additional forms that accompany the IHT400. Use the IHT400 help notes to help you decide which you need to complete.

If you do have Inheritance Tax to pay, you should send forms IHT400 and IHT421 together with any payment of Inheritance Tax, if you've already worked this out, to HMRC. Use the address on the form.

If you've indicated on the form that you'd like HMRC to work out the tax for you they will do this and tell you what is due. Once any tax due has been paid, or if there's no tax to pay,

HMRC will stamp and return the IHT421 to you. You'll need the stamped IHT421 for the probate interview.

You can contact the **Probate and Inheritance Tax Helpline** if you need any advice or help 0300 123 1072.

Applying for a grant without a solicitor

You can apply for a grant without using a solicitor if the deceased was living in Northern Ireland and:

- left a valid Will and you are named as executor in that Will
- Did not leave a Will but you are next of kin and are resident in the UK

To get a grant, you'll need to go to an interview bringing the required original documents with you, confirm the details in your application and sign the probate forms.

Documents and information you'll need

The below are the documents and information needed for the interview:

- photo Id for applicant(s)
- death or coroner's certificate
- inheritance tax form IHT205 or IHT421

- original Will
- marriage certificate – if no Will and the deceased was married
- Decree Absolute – if no Will and the deceased was divorced
- probate fee payment
- other forms required by the Probate Officer

A copy of the Will is not acceptable. Make sure that no-one writes on the original Will or attaches paperclips or staples to it. The original Will is kept in the court file after the interview. The certified copy of the death certificate will also be kept on file at the court.

Requesting an interview appointment

When you have all the documents and information needed, you should send a completed appointment request form with the required copy documents to correct the Probate Office. If the deceased lived in County Fermanagh, Londonderry or Tyrone you can use either the Londonderry or Belfast office, but if they lived in County Antrim, Armagh or Down you must use the Belfast office. If there is no inheritance tax to pay, you should send the following documents with the appointment request form:

- copy of the death certificate

- completed tax form IHT205

- copy of the will - if there is one

If you completed the tax form IHT400 and IHT421, you'll need to send the following:

- copy of the death certificate

- the stamped IHT421 form

- copy of the will - if there is one

The Probate Office will try to give you an interview within three weeks of getting your appointment request form. You will be notified of the appointment date and time by telephone or letter. The interview will take place in a private office and will last about 30 minutes. If an executor named in the deceased's Will cannot come to the interview, you should contact the relevant Probate Office, they will tell you what to do. If the deceased person left a Will, at least seven days must have passed from the date of death to the date of appointment. If there is no Will, 28 days must have passed.

Probate interview

You need to bring the required original documents to the interview. You can bring a friend with you, but no person acting as an adviser may be present at the interview. Probate staff will look at the documents, ask you some questions and prepare the probate forms for you to check. You will make an oath or affirmation confirming that all the details of your application are true and correct. You will then sign the probate forms.

After the interview

The Probate Office should issue the Grant of Probate or Grant of Letters of Administration soon after the interview. It will be sent to you by post.

Probate fees

The fees to be paid are based on the net value of the estate and are made up of two parts, the grant fee and the personal application fee.

(see overleaf)

Net value of the estate	Grant fee	Personal application fee*
less than £10,000	nil	nil
more than £10,000	£237.00	£59.00

*The personal application fee is only charged if you are applying for a grant without a solicitor.

Certified copies of a grant cost £12.00 each. These are useful if you have to deal with several financial institutions.

Now read the key points from Chapter six

Key points from Chapter six

- Probate means that the executor's powers to administer the estate of the dead person have been officially confirmed
- Probate has a number of objectives under the law-to safeguard the creditors of the deceased, to ensure reasonable provision is made for the deceased's dependants and to distribute the balance of the estate in accordance with the intentions of the person whose will it is
- One of the key factors affecting the need to obtain probate is how much money is left under the will
- The process of obtaining probate is different in the various parts of the UK.

Ch. 7

The Intervention of the Courts

_____

Introduction

Where an individual has died without making proper provision in their Will for their relatives or dependants, judges have a wide discretion to redistribute assets to produce a fair result.

Who can apply for an order?

Under the Inheritance (Provision for Family and Dependants) Act 1975 only certain people are entitled to make an application to the court for an order. Broadly speaking, these are the immediate family of the deceased, or their partner if they were living together as husband and wife (or as civil partners).

In order to make an application under the Inheritance Act, the applicant must also show that the deceased was 'domiciled' in England or Wales, which, in very broad terms, means that they were permanently based in this jurisdiction.

When to apply for an order

Any application under the Inheritance Act must be made within six months of the Personal Representatives obtaining a grant of probate to allow them to administer the estate. Outside this time limit, the court's permission will be needed to allow the applicant to begin proceedings. This permission is usually given only in exceptional circumstances.

Grounds for making a claim

There is only one ground for a claim under the Inheritance Act, which is that the disposition (or division) of the deceased's estate, whether following his Will or under the laws of Intestacy, does not make reasonable financial provision for the applicant.

Where the applicant is a spouse, or a civil partner, of the deceased, 'reasonable financial provision' means such provision as would be reasonable in all the circumstances of the case for a husband or wife or a civil partner to receive, whether or not that provision is required for his or her maintenance. The court must consider, but is not bound to follow, the likely settlement that would have made within divorce proceedings, if the parties had divorced rather than the deceased having died. You may hear this referred to as the 'divorce fiction'. For all other applicants under the Inheritance

Act, 'reasonable financial provision' means such provision as it would be reasonable in all the circumstance of the case for the applicant to receive for his maintenance. Thus the court will not make an order in these circumstances only because the applicant feels that the Will or Intestacy is unfair or is not as they expected. The applicant must show that he had a reasonable expectation of having his living costs met by the deceased. If the applicant was financially independent of the deceased before the date of death, it may be very difficult to show such an expectation.

Orders the court can make

The judge has a wide discretion to redistribute assets to provide a fair result. The court can make any of the following orders:-

a) an order that the applicant should receive regular payments (known as 'periodical payments') from the net estate of the deceased, for as much and for as long as the judge considers reasonable.

b) an order that the applicant should receive a single lump sum payment from the estate.

c) an order that a property owned by the deceased be transferred to the applicant.

d) an order for the settlement of any property for the benefit of the applicant ie. an order creating a trust for the applicant

e) an order for the purchase of property using assets of the estate, and for such property either to be transferred to the applicant or to be held in trust for his benefit.

f) an order varying any pre- or post-nuptial (or pre- or post-civil partnership) settlement to which the deceased was a party, for the benefit of a surviving spouse or civil partner, or for a child or step-child of the deceased.

In cases where the court is satisfied that the applicant is in immediate need of financial assistance, but it is not yet possible to reach a final decision about the order that should be made, and the court is satisfied that there are assets available to meet the applicant's immediate needs, the court also has jurisdiction to make 'interim' orders for a payment or payments from the estate. Any such payments may be taken into account when a final order is made.

Factors The Court Must Consider

In deciding whether to make an order under the Inheritance Act, the court must first decide whether the Will of the deceased, or the laws of Intestacy, make reasonable financial provision for the applicant, and only if such provision has not been made, whether and in what manner it should exercise its powers to make one of

118

the above orders. The specific factors that the court must by law consider when deciding these questions are as follows:-

1. the financial resources and financial needs which the applicant has or is likely to have in the foreseeable future;

2. the financial resources and financial needs which any other applicant for an order under the Inheritance Act from the estate of the deceased has or is likely to have in the foreseeable future;

3. the financial resources and financial needs which any beneficiary of the estate of the deceased has or is likely to have in the foreseeable future;

4. any obligations and responsibilities which the deceased had towards any applicant for an order or towards any beneficiary of his estate;

5. the size and nature of the net estate of the deceased

6. any physical or mental disability of any applicant or any beneficiary of the estate

7. any other matter, including the conduct of the applicant or any other person, which in the circumstances of the case the court may consider relevant.

In cases where the applicant is a spouse or civil partner, the court must also consider those factors given weight within divorce proceedings, such as the length of the marriage, or civil partnership, the contributions made by the parties to the family's welfare and the age of the applicant.

In cases where the applicant is a child or step-child of the deceased, the court will also consider the manner in which the applicant is being, or is expected to be, educated or trained. With step-children, the court will further look at the extent to which the deceased had taken on responsibility for the child's maintenance, whether any other person had a duty to maintain the child and whether the deceased, in taking responsibility for the child, was aware that she/he was not the natural parent. In cases where a claim is brought by a person being maintained by the deceased at the time of his death, the court will look at the extent to which, and the basis upon which, the deceased began maintaining the applicant and the length of time for which he had done so.

The Procedure

The procedure for Inheritance Act applications is governed by the Civil Procedure Rules. These are designed to assist litigants and to ensure that all cases are run as efficiently as possible, without incurring unnecessary legal costs. However, before issuing any application, your solicitor will wish to discuss with you the possibility of using a process of out of court Dispute Resolution (DR). This may involve mediation or 'round table' negotiations, and is intended to assist the parties to reach a fair compromise, without involving the courts. Only if DR is inappropriate to your case, or is unsuccessful in settling your claim, will your solicitor advise you to issue court proceedings.

If you decide to issue proceedings, a claim form will be sent to the court, along with supporting documents where appropriate. These give details to the court of the basis of your application. Once issued, the claim and any supporting documentation will be served upon the defendants. The court will normally list a preliminary hearing, at which a number of directions may be given. These may include permission to the parties to file any evidence upon which they wish to rely, and orders to disclose any information or documents in their possession which may be relevant to the proceedings. The defendants will usually be given the opportunity to set out their arguments against your claim in a written 'Defence'.

Once all these documents have been filed, the court may list a further hearing, which is an opportunity for the judge and the parties to check that all directions have been complied with, all relevant information has been provided, and to set a timetable to move the case forward. The exact procedure for this stage of your case will vary depending upon the details of your claim, and your solicitor will advise you about this in more detail as appropriate. It is essential that you abide by any timetable or deadlines given by the court, as failure to do so may be prejudicial to your case.

There is an ongoing duty upon the parties to continue to negotiate even after proceedings have been issued. Failure to do so may be reflected in the eventual order in relation to costs, if the matter proceeds to final hearing. If the parties have failed to reach an agreement, and once the court is satisfied that all necessary information is available, the matter will be listed for final hearing. At this hearing, the judge will normally want all parties to give evidence, and may also want to hear evidence from any experts witnesses involved. After hearing this evidence, the judge will decide whether to make an order as outlined above.

Legal costs

Any agreement reached on financial provision should also provide for the payment of each party's legal costs. It is common for each party's costs to be met from the estate of the deceased if agreement is reached, although this is not always the case. If the matter proceeds to a final hearing, then the judge will decide, after making the final orders, what orders for costs to make. This could mean that each party pays their own costs, or one party pays the other's.

❖

Ch.8

Welfare Benefits after Bereavement

Bereavement benefits if you were married or in a civil partnership

Bereavement benefits are for people whose husband, wife or civil partner has died. Which benefits and how much you qualify for will depend on:

- Your age
- Whether you have dependent children
- Whether the person who died paid enough National Insurance Contributions during their working lives.

Changes to bereavement benefits from April 2017

From 6 April 2017, these bereavement benefits have been replaced by Bereavement Support Payment:

- Bereavement Payment
- Bereavement Allowance
- Widowed Parent's Allowance.

However, Bereavement Payment, Bereavement Allowance and Widowed Parent's Allowance can be backdated for up to three months. So if your spouse or civil partner died on or before 5 April 2017, you might still be able to claim them if you qualify and apply within three months of the date of their death. If you're currently getting Bereavement Allowance or Widowed Parent's Allowance, you will continue to receive them for the time being.

What is Bereavement Support Payment?

If your spouse or civil partner died on or after 6 April 2017, you might be eligible to get Bereavement Support Payment to help you cope financially. The benefit is paid to you at one of two rates depending on whether you are responsible for children. You must be below State Pension Age to claim Bereavement Support Payment. Your spouse or civil partner must have made enough National Insurance Contributions during their working life for you to qualify. Bereavement Support Payment is only paid for 18 months after the date when your spouse or civil partner died so it's important you claim as soon as possible to avoid losing money.

How much is Bereavement Support Payment?

Bereavement Support Payment is paid at either a higher rate or standard rate:

126

Higher rate

Paid to pregnant women or if you're entitled to Child Benefit. You'll get:

- A monthly payment of £350 for 18 months following the death.
- A one-off payment of £3,500 during the first month.

Standard rate

For everyone else. You'll get:

- A monthly payment of £100 for 18 months.
- A one-off payment of £2,500 during the first month.

You might also be eligible to claim other low income benefits to top up your income, like tax credits, Housing Benefit, Council Tax Reduction or Universal Credit.

How do I claim Bereavement Support Payment?

You can claim from the date when the person dies. Claims can be backdated up to three months only. So make sure you make your claim within three months of your spouse or civil partner's death or you might lose some of your payments.

Call the Bereavement Service helpline or pick up a form at your local JobCentre Plus.

Bereavement Service helpline

Telephone: 0800 731 0469
Welsh language: 0800 731 0453
Textphone: 0800 731 0464
Welsh language: 0800 731 0456

Monday to Friday, 8am to 6pm

Bereavement benefits if you were living together

You can't claim bereavement benefits if you were living together but weren't married or in a civil partnership. But you can try applying for other benefits, such as:

- Income Support
- Housing Benefit
- Universal credit, or
- Working Tax Credit

How to claim benefits if you're on a low income

If you're facing a drop in income after your partner dies, you might be able to claim a range of benefits to top up your income and help with things like housing costs or bringing up children. Some benefits are means-tested. This means any savings or income you have will affect whether you are entitled to benefit payments. This includes an inheritance taking your savings over the £16,000 threshold. Try to report the death as soon as you can. This will help you get the benefits you're entitled to as quickly as possible. To do this, you'll need to let the Department for Work and Pensions (DWP) know the person has died.

Tell Us Once

If you live in England, Scotland or Wales you can contact the Tell Us Once service to cancel the deceased's benefits and entitlements. The Tell Us Once service is a government service, offered by most local authorities which also inform the DVLA, HMRC, Passport Office and local council for you and check if you're eligible for help with funeral costs or other benefits.

Funeral Payment

If you're on a low income and struggling to pay for a funeral for your partner, you can apply for a Funeral Payment. If the person who died left money, you will usually need to pay back any amount you received through the Funeral Payments scheme.

How much you will get

The amount you get depends on your circumstances, but could be up to £700 towards funeral expenses plus payments to cover the costs of things like burial or cremation fees.

How your bereavement benefits affect other benefits

If you claim any of the following benefits, your payments might be affected if you start getting Bereavement Support Payment or are getting Bereavement Allowance or Widowed Parent's Allowance.

- Universal Credit
- Income Support
- Incapacity Benefit
- Jobseeker's Allowance
- Carer's Allowance
- Employment and Support Allowance
- Pension Credit (only if you receive Bereavement Allowance)

Bereavement Payment or the lump sum you get as part of Bereavement Support Payment counts as savings when your entitlement to some means-tested benefits is worked out. This

130

means if you get the one-off lump sum payment, you might see a reduction in the following benefits:

- Income Support
- Housing Benefit
- Income-based Jobseeker's Allowance
- Employment and Support Allowance
- Universal Credit

To find out more about how other benefits might be affected, contact the Bereavement Service, which is run by the Pension Service of the Department of Work and Pensions (DWP):

- If you live in England and Wales, call 0345 606 0265).
- For the Welsh language helpline, call 0345 606 0275).
- If you live in Northern Ireland, call 0800 085 2463 (free to call).

Benefits calculators

There are a number of benefit calculators which can help you work out what you're entitled to. For a general idea of the benefits you might be eligible for, use the Citizens Advice benefit calculator. For a more detailed breakdown of what you might get, use the Turn2us benefit calculator, or the Entitled to benefit calculator .

Tax and National Insurance

Your income will probably change after the death of your husband, wife or civil partner. If you get extra money from pensions, annuities, benefits or an inheritance, you may need to pay more tax. You may be on a lower income and need to pay less tax. Your tax allowances - the income you do not pay tax on - may also change.

Income you must report

Tell HMRC if you get:

- interest from a bank, building society or a National Savings and Investment product, eg pensioner income, capital bonds
- income from letting out property
- income from Purchased Life Annuities
- Widowed Parent's Allowance or Bereavement Allowance
- Carer's Allowance
- foreign pension payments
- other income that should have been taxed but has not been

You do not need to tell HMRC about:

- income your employer pays tax on through PAYE
- income from a private pension
- income which does not get taxed, eg from an Individual Savings Account (ISA)
- any income if you'll reach State Pension age within 4 months
- getting Jobseeker's Allowance (JSA), Incapacity Benefit, Employment and Support Allowance (ESA) or Bereavement Support Payment

Tax allowances

If you pay Income Tax, you'll have a **Personal Allowance** - income you do not pay tax on. Your allowance may change if your income changes. HMRC will automatically adjust your Personal Allowance when you tell them about your change of income.

Married Couple's Allowance

If you or your husband, wife or civil partner were born before 6 April 1935, you may have been claiming Married Couple's Allowance. You'll still get the allowance for the current tax year (up to 5 April) but HMRC will automatically stop it after that and you'll get just your Personal Allowance.

Blind Person's Allowance

If your husband, wife or civil partner was claiming Blind Person's Allowance, ask HMRC to transfer what's left of their Blind Person's Allowance for the current tax year (up to 5 April) to you.

HMRC Blind Person's Allowance enquiries

Telephone: 0300 200 3301

Monday to Friday, 8am to 8pm

Saturday, 8am to 4pm

Reduced rate National Insurance

If you're a widow and you were married before April 1977, you might be paying a reduced rate of National Insurance (sometimes called the 'small stamp'). You may be able to keep paying the reduced rate. Contact HMRC to find out what you should do.

Pensions

You may be able to get extra pension payments from your husband, wife or civil partner's pension or National Insurance contributions.

State Pension

You need to be over State Pension age to claim extra payments from your husband, wife or civil partner's State Pension. What you get and how you claim will depend on whether you reached State Pension age before or after 6 April 2016. Contact the Pension Service to check what you can claim. www.gov.uk/contact-pension-service. This site will also give guidance on the process in Scotland and Northern Irenad.

If you reached State Pension age before 6 April 2016

You'll get any State Pension based on your husband, wife or civil partner's National Insurance contribution when you claim your own pension. You will not get it if you remarry or form a new civil partnership before you reach State Pension age.

If you reached State Pension age on or after 6 April 2016

You'll receive the 'new State Pension' and you may be able to inherit an extra payment on top of your pension.

Private pensions

You may get payments from your husband, wife or civil partner's workplace, personal or stakeholder pension - it will depend on the pension scheme. Contact the pension scheme to find out. You'll have to pay tax on those payments if the pension provider does not pay it for you.

War Widow's or Widower's Pension

You may be able to get War Widow's or Widower Pension - if your husband, wife or civil partner died because of their service in the Armed Forces or because of a war.

Financial help if your husband, wife or civil partner was in the Armed Forces

If your husband, wife or civil partner died as a result of serving in the Armed Forces, you may be able to get financial help from Veterans UK 0808 1914 218. It does not matter whether your husband, wife or civil partner died during active service or not, as long as the death was caused by service in the Armed Forces. You may get a War Widow's or War Widower's pension, or a guaranteed income payment (based on your spouse or civil partner's earnings), depending on when the injury, illness or death was caused. You can get more information on guaranteed income payments, the war pension scheme and the Armed Forces Compensation Scheme on GOV.UK.

Useful Addresses

There are a number of agencies that provide help to those who have experienced bereavement. Below is a list of the key agencies with addresses, phone numbers and in most cases e mails.

Age UK

England

Tavis House

1-6 Tavistock Square

London

WC1H 9NA

0800 055 6112

E mail contact:@ageuk.org.uk

Scotland

Causeway House

160 Causewayside

Edinburgh EH9 1PR

Tel: 0333 3232 400

info@agescotland.org.uk

Northern Ireland

3 Lower Crescent

Belfast BT7 1NR

0808 808 7575 8am-7am (365 days a year)

info@ageni.org

Wales

Age Cymru,
Ground Floor, Mariners House,
Trident Court,
East Moors Road,
Cardiff, CF24 5TD.
Tel: 029 2043 1555

www.ageuk.org.uk/cymru

Asian Funeral Service (Leicester Branch)

260 Loughborough Road

LE54 5LH

0116 319 8232

Cruse-Bereavement Care

PO Box 800

Richmond, TW9 1RG

Tel: 0808 808 1677

info@cruse.org.uk

Foundation for the Study of Infant Death (The Lullaby Trust)

11 Belgrave Road

London SW1V 1RB

Tel: 0207 802 3200

office@lullabytrust.org.uk

Funeral Planning Authority

Barham Court

Teston

Maidestone Kent

0845 601 9619 www.funeralplanning authority.com

Institute of Family Therapy

24-32 Stephenson Way

London NW1 2HX

Tel: 0207 391 9150

Fax: 0207 391 9169

www.ift.org.uk

Jewish Bereavement Counseling Service

c/o Maurice and Vivienne Wohl Campus

221 Golders Green Road

London

NW11 9DQ

0208 951 3881

enquiries@jbcs.org.uk

National Association of Funeral Directors

618 Warwick Road

Solihull

West Midlands B91 1AA

0121 711 1343

www.nafd.org.uk

National Association of Memorial Masons

1 Castle Mews

Rugby, CV21 2XL

Tel: 01788 542 264

www.namm.org.uk

Index

*